WILL vs. TRUST

CORE ESTATE PLANNING CONCEPTS EXPLAINED

BY

JOHN KENT KIDWELL, ESQ.

ABOUT THE AUTHOR

John Kidwell is the Owner and President of the Law Firm of Kidwell & Kent, with offices in Fairfax, Virginia, and Rockville, Maryland. Mr. Kidwell also owns and operates his in-firm commercial and residential real estate title company, Old Dominion Title Services, Inc.

In 2013 John was selected by the Heritage Registry of Who's Who as a pillar of the community for his work as an attorney and continued dedication to charitable contributions.

In 2014 John was inducted as a member of Trial Masters, an elite national organization composed of lawyers with significant courtroom experience. Membership is an indication of a strong commitment to taking clients' cases all the way to the courthouse when warranted. Fewer than 1/2 of 1% of the attorneys in the United States are members.

In 2015, Mr. Kidwell was peer nominated and awarded through the Heritage Foundation as a top attorney in the nation.

In 2016, the Expert Network certified Mr. Kidwell in the TOP 3% of attorneys in America.

In 2017 John obtained his Life Health and Annuities, Series 7 and Series 66 securities licenses to provide individual and business financial planning services to his clients.

In 2018 Mr. Kidwell was peer nominated and awarded as a top Estate Planning Attorney in America by Lawyers of Distinction.

Mr. Kidwell is a published author on the topic of law and politics. His books, "Leading by Example: Renovating the American Dream", and "25 Articles on the Law", can be found on Amazon and are available for download.

John's Law Firm of Kidwell & Kent is a general practice law firm with many areas of legal concentration. Mr. Kidwell has over 15 years in real estate litigation and transactions, wills, trusts and estate planning, business and corporate law, family and domestic relations, civil litigation, personal injury, and financial planning.

John received his bachelor of Arts in Political Science from the University of Mary Washington and his juris doctorate from the University of George Mason School of Law.

John always keeps philanthropy at the forefront of his endeavors. In 2006 he founded Alternative Fuels for America, a 501©(3) charitable organization designed to raise money for the National Renewable Energy Laboratory in order to fund the advancement of clean fuel technologies and alternative energy sources, specifically for automobiles.

In 2011, Mr. Kidwell was a Man of the Year candidate for the Leukemia & Lymphoma Society, raising funds for a cure for cancer.

Mr. Kidwell regularly conducts free legal clinics for Wills for Heroes, the Veterans Administration, local churches and assisted living facilities.

John was appointed by the Fairfax County Board of Supervisors to the Information Technology Policy Advisory Committee, tasked with advising local government on the implementation and management of information technology services and platforms. Mr. Kidwell served on the Information Policy Advisory Committee from 2011-2013.

Mr. Kidwell is also a member of the Fairfax Rotary and has served as the Membership Services Coordinator. John has even performed as outside counsel for the Fairfax County Republican Committee and multiple Congressional campaigns, as well as served on the Fairfax Legislative Committee since 2006.

TABLE OF CONTENTS

CHAPTER 1:   ASSET TRANSFER PYRAMID

CHAPTER 2:   WHEN YOU ONLY NEED A WILL

CHAPTER 3:   WHEN DO I NEED A TRUST?

CHAPTER 4:   TRANSFER ON DEATH DEED

CHAPTER 5:   ADVANCE MEDICAL DIRECTIVE

CHAPTER 6:   DURABLE POWER OF ATTORNEY

CHAPTER 1:

THE ASSET TRANSFER PYRAMID

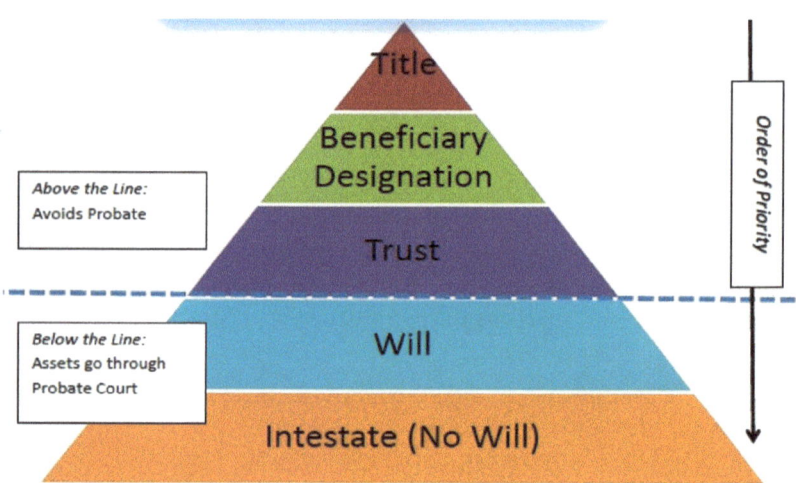

The key to understanding how an estate plan is meant to function, centers around the understanding of how property of all kinds pass at death. The asset transfer pyramid illustrates the order of priority the law affords designations for assets and what governs the disposition of those assets upon the death of their owner.

Everything that someone owns when they die becomes their estate. Clothes, furniture, cars, checking accounts, savings accounts, retirement accounts, life insurance policies, and real estate, etc. - all of this adds up to the sum total of our estate at death.

No matter who you are, all assets held in your estate pass in the order of priority shown in the asset transfer pyramid; to-wit: 1. Title; 2: (Contract) Beneficiary Designation; 3. Trust; 4 Will; 5: Intestate.

The goal of any estate is to make sure that all assets pass to the intended beneficiaries with the least amount of cost, and legal hassle to the beneficiaries or the people you appoint to carry out your desires as to the disposition of your estate.

In some cases, a simple Last Will & Testament is sufficient as the foundation of an individual's estate plan, as all assets potentially in the estate can be designated to pass by title or contract. In some instances, it is not possible, or advisable to have an asset pass by title or contract, and therefore, a Revocable Living Trust Agreement (Trust) becomes necessary to adequately provide for the cost effective and efficient transfer of estate assets.

TITLE: Often times there are joint owners of a particular asset. For instance, husband and wife may own a joint bank account or their home as joint owners with common law right of survivorship. This means that, at the death of the first co-owner, the surviving joint owner, by operation of common law, becomes the sole owner or the subject asset.

I often quip with my clients… If your house is titled jointly with your spouse, you could name me as the beneficiary, and thank you, but I'm not going to get it. Title takes precedence over a Last Will and Testament.

CONTRACT: Not all accounts are jointly titled. Many people are single, or their spouse has predeceased. In fact, some accounts are solely titled by their very nature, such as Individual Retirement Accounts (IRAs) and Life Insurance Policies. How do those assets pass to your progeny?

The answer, is Contract. Specifically, beneficiary designations on each and every financial asset that you own.

Chances are you're familiar with beneficiary designations. Anybody who has an IRA, 401(k), Life Insurance policy, or any other account the IRS has designated as a "Qualified Account" -because these types of accounts qualify for special tax treatment under the Internal Revenue Code- has been required to fill out a beneficiary designation form. The Internal Revenue Code requires that beneficiary designations, along with vesting schedules, etc. be part of the establishment of any qualified account.

The beneficiary designation is a contract between you and the manager/holder of that account, that simply states upon proof of your death, the manger/holder of your account is to pay the value of the asset over to the named beneficiary in the percentages delineated.

Yet, not all accounts are qualified accounts. It is also imperative to establish contracts for the disposition of your checking, savings, and investments accounts that don't qualify for tax deferrals or tax free status. In 15 years of being an attorney, I've had about 3 people come in and say that they've already named beneficiaries on their checking account. The reason for this is because the IRS does not require these types of accounts to have beneficiary designations, as they are not "qualified" accounts. As such, banks and other institutions simply view the designation contracts as more paperwork, and don't ask or require they be completed.

Another heads up: on checking and savings accounts, instead of calling the contracts beneficiary designations, they are called payable on death designations (P.O.D) or transfer on death designations (T.O.D.) This is basically interchangeable terminology. Think about the definition of a beneficiary = somebody to whom you pay or transfer an asset upon death of the owner.

There are limitations, however, to naming beneficiaries in a contract. What if the beneficiary predeceases you? What if they are under the age of 18? What if they are incapacitated? What if...

CHAPTER 2:
WHEN YOU ONLY NEED A WILL

The best way to think of a Last Will and Testament ("Will") is as the catch-net of your estate.

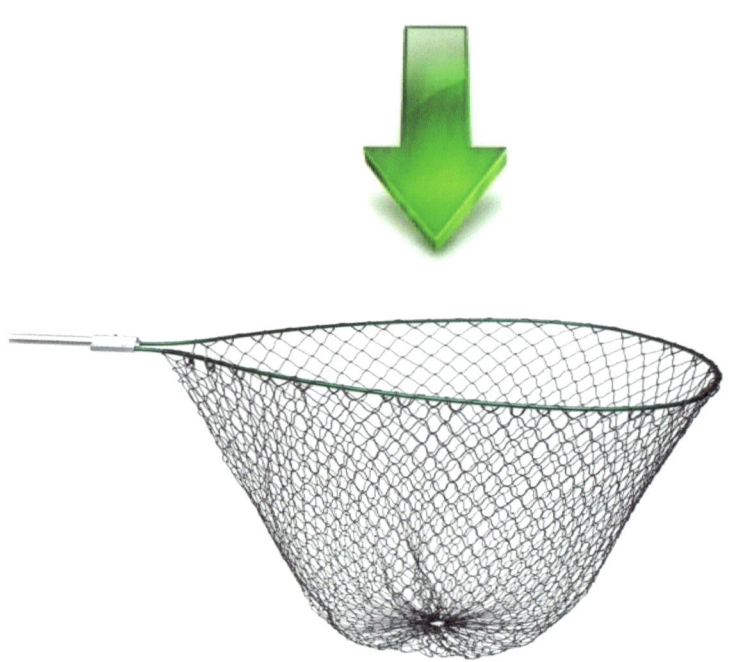

A Last Will & Testament is just that, a "Last" line of defense, to make sure nothing slips through the cracks. That being said, even though everyone needs a Will, I never want a Will to catch anything in anybody's estate. Why? Probate.

Probate is the Latin word for prove. It means to prove your will. That is the easy part, because of the way wills are executed. They almost always are accompanied by a self-proving affidavit, which states that the will was signed by the testator in the presence of two witnesses, who in turn signed in the presence of a notary public. This means that the Executor (the person named in a will to "execute" the terms of the will) does not have to track down witnesses who are long gone and may themselves be dead.

But when people say "avoid probate" what they really mean is- avoid the administration of your estate through the court system.

If an asset is caught in the catch-net of your estate, your will, then your Executor must administer the estate through the probate division of the circuit court of the county in which you lived at the time of your death.

In a nutshell, the probate process is as follows:

- ✓ The Executor must appear before the probate clerk with your original will, original death certificate, proof of their identity and a check. The check is for the probate court fee, which is based upon a published table of value of assets passing through the estate.
- ✓ The Executor must qualify before the court to receive letters testamentary and a certificate of qualification, and then post a bond and/or surety for the faithful performance of their duties.
- ✓ Within 30 days, the Executor must notify all heirs at law that they have qualified as Executor, and file an affidavit with the probate clerk, affirming they have sent said notifications. A fee is assessed by the probate clerk at this juncture.
- ✓ Within 4 months of qualification as Executor, the Executor must prepare an inventory of assets with proof of value as the date of death of the decedent, and file the inventory with the Commissioner of Accounts Office. The COA assesses a fee for intake and review of the estate inventory.
- ✓ The Will becomes a matter of public record.
- ✓ The Executor pays the Commissioner of Accounts Office to hold a debts and demands hearing and send a notice in the classified section of a newspaper of common circulation in the area, notifying all potential creditors that should they have any claim, they must come to the COA's office on the stated hearing date, or forever hold their peace. The Commission of Accounts Office and the newspaper assess fees for this service.
- ✓ Within 16 months of qualifying as Executor, the Executor must file an Accounting with the Commissioner of Accounts office, hopefully showing the disbursements to beneficiaries, receipts, account statements, debits, credits, and a zero balance. The COA assesses yet another fee, but, if the COA

approves the account, and it is the final account, the estate is finally closed.

✓ The sunken cost to an estate passing through the courts, via a Last Will and Testament, is are often $10,000 - $30,000, dependent upon the size of the estate.

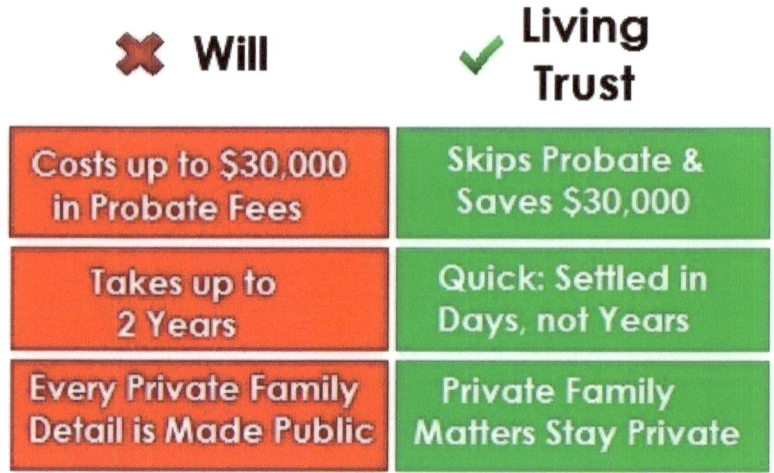

For the reasons above delineated, the administration of any estate through the court system, aka "probate" should be avoided like the bubonic plague.

However, a will does serve its purposes, and for many estates, it is more than sufficient to meet the needs of the maker.

If a client can be coached to update all of their beneficiary designations on all financial assets, none of their beneficiaries are minors, they have no reservations about leaving lump sums to their beneficiaries, with no strings attached, and the client does not own real estate in multiple states, or own an interest in a closely held business, such as an LLC, a Last Will and Testament is probably more than sufficient for their estate planning needs. In short, I create a will for the client, with the hopes that it will never need to be used.

To understand this, it is incumbent upon me to explain further how a will works.

Most people, when thinking of a will, understand what it is, generically. A will is a document in which you state where you want your assets to go when you die. And while that is correct, there is more to it than that.

You might be thinking, okay, in my will, I need to specifically state that I want my real estate located at 525 make believe avenue to go to my wife, and my account with bank account #xx5 shall go to… The truth is, no, not really. While you can provide for specific bequests in a will, it is not advisable, and the function of a will, being the catch-net of your estate, means that wills are actually more generic than you might think.

Instead, wills state that you "do hereby give, devise and bequeath the rest residue and remainder of your estate, of whatsoever nature, and wheresoever situate, unto…" This is what we call the residuary clause of your will, and it is generic because we don't know what assets you will have in 1 year, let alone 20 years from now.

People move, they change accounts, and they don't want to have to change their estate plan every time they open an account. As such, a will is designed as the catch-net of your estate.

The question that then presents itself is, okay, then what constitutes the rest residue and remainder of my estate? What does the residuary clause of my will govern?

The Answer: The residue of your estate is any asset that has not been designated to pass by title or by contract (beneficiary designation).

CHAPTER 3:
WHEN DO I NEED A TRUST?

As I said in chapter 2, if a client can be coached to update all of their beneficiary designations on all financial assets, none of their beneficiaries are minors, they have no reservations about leaving lump sums to their beneficiaries, with no strings attached, and the client does not own real estate in multiple states, or own an interest in a closely held business, such as an LLC, a Last Will and Testament is probably more than sufficient for their estate planning needs. In short, I create a will for the client, with the hopes that it will never need to be used.

However, there are many situations that call for a trust being necessary.

First off, what is a Trust? A trust trust is a contract between the Grantor/maker of the Trust (individual or family/business) and the Trustee (manager of the Trust), that reads much like a Last Will and Testament, granting the Trustee managerial powers and instructing the Trustee to disburse the assets transferred into the trust as directed in the contract.

Specifically, a living trust, also called an inter vivos (between the living) or revocable trust, is an estate planning tool increasingly used by individuals and families of all income brackets as a way to pass on property while generally avoiding costs and delays associated with probate.

There are many reasons why trusts can become advisable, to include special needs, corporate interests, etc., but the most prevalent and important reason why people get trusts, is to avoid probate.

If an asset is owned by the trust, the trust governs what happens to that asset at the death of the grantor of the trust, and the asset is not subject to probate.

The key is that a trust must be funded. A trust can say, in the most beautiful legal prose, that Asset A goes to beneficiary X, but the Trust only governs that which it owns. This is because a trust, boiled down to its roots, is really just a fancy stack of paper; a fictitious entity, just like a corporation. It only governs that which it owns.

How do we fund a trust? With all financial assets: checking and savings accounts, retirement accounts, life insurance policies… you must name your trust as the beneficiary of the asset upon your death.

Real estate is titled into the trust via a recorded deed transferring the property into the Trust at present, or via a Revocable Transfer on Death Deed (discussed in Chapter 4).

Personal assets, such as clothes, furniture, jewelry, and cars, are listed in the Schedule A attached and incorporated into the trust. With personal property, referred to at law as chattels, it is sufficient to simply state that they are funded into the trust. This is sufficient at law because it is understood that it isn't practical to put sticky notes on your earrings stating they are owned by your trust. However, with real estate and financial assets, the requirement at law is that you do something more affirmative to fund the trust; to-wit: Beneficiary Designations and the Revocable Transfer on Death Deed.

Okay, so when would I need a Trust?

Do you have children or any beneficiaries under the age of 18? Any contract that designates a minor as the beneficiary, is considered void at law, should you die before your beneficiary turns 18. Therefore, your child's beneficial share in, say, your IRA, would fail, and not pass by title or by contract. Not having passed by title or contract, that IRA will fall into the catch-net of your estate – your Last Will and Testament.

While the assets will get to your child, your estate will now be subject to probate, and the costs and delays resulting therefrom.

Also, you may not want your child to receive hundreds of thousands of dollars at age 18. They might be the most responsible young adults, but financially, at 18, they are financially ignorant. Your kid might be the one paying for keg parties as opposed to going to class, or traveling through Europe to find themselves instead of enrolling. In a Trust, you can state that your child does not receive the assets until the age of 25, or graduation from a post-secondary degree institution, for instance. Whereas, in a beneficiary designation contract, you cannot put any limitations. If a beneficiary is named and they are at least 18 when you die, they get the money outright with no strings attached and you can't govern from the grave.

Alternatively, parents with minor children, should set up a Single Family Revocable Living Trust Agreement, and fund it with their assets upon their death, via beneficiary designations for financial assets, and a Revocable Transfer on Death Deed for their real estate. By doing so, all assets are controlled by a Successor Trustee named in the Trust (hypothetically, let's call her Aunt Susie), and once you pass on, day one, Aunt Susie has the powers to manage the trust assets for the health, maintenance, education and welfare of your children and other beneficiaries, in the exact manner prescribed as your wishes. Most importantly, because the subject assets passed by contract, via beneficiary designation, into the trust, probate is avoided.

When you own real estate, it is often advisable to have a trust.

The passage of real estate is governed by the title to the property, also known as the deed. Between joint owners, such as husband

and wife, who own with common law right of survivorship, there is no issue with the home passing smoothly to the survivor spouse because it occurs automatically, as a matter of common law.

But, what happens when the survivor between the joint owners later dies? Or what if husband and wife die in a common accident? How does their real estate pass to their children, or other beneficiaries?

Again, the answer is found in title.

If the children are under the age of 18, the parents should execute a revocable transfer on death deed, vesting title to the real estate in the family trust, upon the death of both parents. Then, immediately upon the death of the surviving parent, Aunt Susie, the Successor Trustee, has the power to manage the real estate, lease it, or sell it and deposit the proceeds into the trust for the benefit of the children.

If the children are all over the age of 18, and let's say, 25 and above, and the parents have no qualms with leaving their assets to their children, directly, with no strings attached, then they can execute a revocable transfer on death deed, designating the children as the beneficiaries of the real estate at their death.

One concern does arise when multiple children suddenly become joint owners of their parent's home the day after their parents die. Often, even if they get along well, there are disagreements as to how to best dispose of the property. Some may have sentimental ties to the home, and may even want to buy out the others, while others may want to simply sell the property and split the proceeds as quickly as possible. When these disagreements occur, they can often be messy and no child has authority over the other to make final decisions. As such, legal battles can ensue, to include suits for the partition of property.

Whereas, alternatively, if those same parents were to name a trust as the beneficiary of the revocable transfer on death deed,

Aunt Susie, as Successor Trustee, immediately, has the sole power and authority to sell the home to one child at fair market value, or to a third party.

Additionally, when a client owns multiple pieces of real estate, such as a rental home in an LLC, and in multiple states, a trust becomes critical.

A trust can grant the trustee the power to wind down and act as the operator of a Limited Liability Company (LLC), owned by someone at the time of their death. Funding the trust with the LLC avoids probate of the assets of an individual's closely held business.

If someone owns real estate in multiple states, and their real estate is governed by their Last Will and Testament, their estate will be subject to what is known as ancillary administration. This means that their estate will have to be probated in each state real estate was owned, further complicating the estate and exacerbating probate costs.

There are many other situations in which a trust can become advisable, such as when there is a special needs child, or incapacitated or spendthrift adult in the family; having an ownership interest in a company; and to establish a charity, to name a few.

CHAPTER 4:
TRANSFER ON DEATH DEED

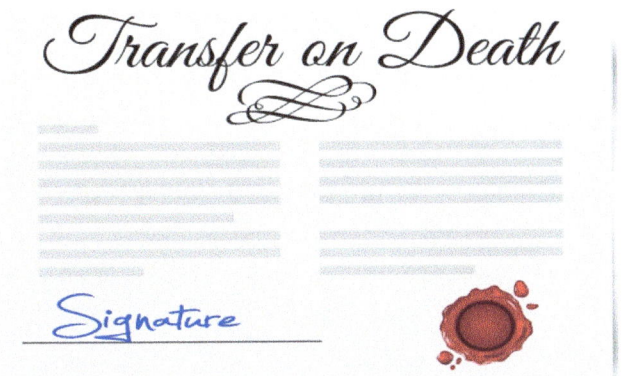

One of the largest assets anyone has when they die is their real estate. It is common for a primary residence to be a nest egg and serve as the foundation of someone's estate. This is why the Revocable Transfer on Death Deeds are critical to any estate plan.

A Revocable Transfer on Death Deed (RTODD) is a real estate deed that is designed to give you the power to designate a beneficiary of each piece of real estate. By the terms of an RTODD, a named beneficiary or beneficiaries, whether they be individuals, or a trust, become the beneficial owners of the subject real estate upon the death of the owner or owners of the property.

An RTODD is easily revocable. In fact, the predicate of the property actually transferring to the beneficiary is that the grantor still owns the subject real estate at death. If you don't own the property when you die, you have already transferred title to some other third party, automatically, by its own terms, revoking the RTODD.

Further, one could imagine a scenario where one might want to change the beneficiary they want to name for their real estate.

As such, the revocable nature of an RTODD is a necessary convenience.

With an RTODD your real estate passes outside of your probate estate, saving your family many thousands of dollars, and years of accountings and court appearances. Because an RTODD names a beneficiary directly, and ensures your real estate passes by title, no will is necessary to figure out where your property is designated to go at your death. The state, which is who is concerned where your property goes when you die, does not need to look to your will, as you've already recorded the RTODD among the land records in the county in which the property is located, published to the world where the real estate passes at your death.

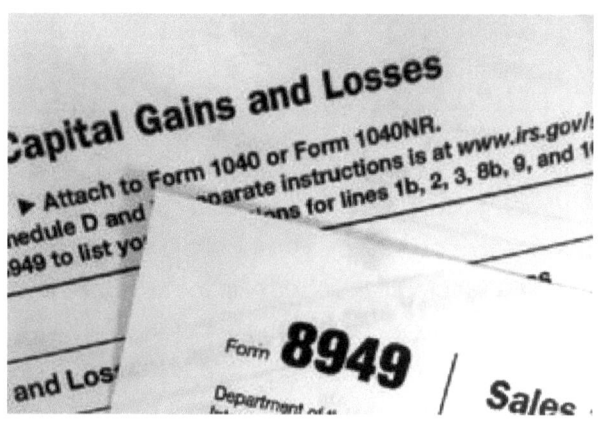

Lastly, an RTODD retains a very important tax savings strategy in any estate plan. Because the beneficiary of an RTODD receives the real estate at the death of the grantor, the beneficiary of the property receives a stepped-up cost basis in the real estate.

Let's say you purchased a home for $200,000 ten years ago. Now, when you die, it is worth $300,000. Your beneficiary of the RTODD now has a cost basis that steps up to the value of the property at the date of your death. This means that when your beneficiary turns around and sells the property to a third party, they would not be paying capital gains taxes on the sale of the property on anything over $200,000 (the grantor's original cost basis), but instead would pay capital gains taxes only to the extent the property sold for greater than $300,000 (the value of the house at the Grantor's death). As a result, thousands are saved in taxes.

CHAPTER 5:
ADVANCE MEDICAL DIRECTIVE

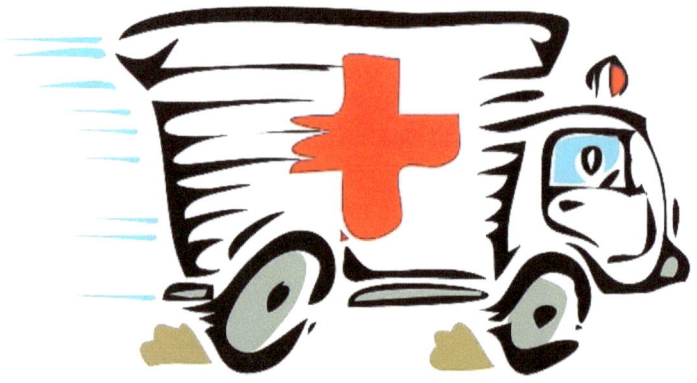

The Advance Medical Directive is a two part document. The first part of the document is called the "Living Will." Unfortunately, a lot of people get the Living Will confused with the Last Will and Testament. They are completely different documents. Sorry – I didn't come up with these terms.

In a Living Will, the maker states that should an attending physician determine that providing life- saving support would do nothing further than to artificially prolong the maker's death, then to withhold treatment, except for the provision of pain killing medication, so that they may die comfortably.

Some people, for religious or other reasons, do not want the Living Will, in which case they should execute a Medical Power of Attorney.

Also, it is important to note that a Living Will is not a Do Not Resuscitate Order (DRO). A DRO is a document you would have on file with your general physician that states you do not wish to be resuscitated should you cease breathing. A DRO is something you would want to have only if you are of advanced years and your standard of living is so deteriorated, that you do not want to be revived should you code.

A Living Will, on the other hand, covers the scenario where you are hit by a car crossing the street, for instance. Your head hits the ground, and the ambulance comes and the doctors do all they can to stabilize you. But, its been weeks and the only thing keeping you alive is your breathing tube and feeding apparatus. If you want all of your money to go to your family, as opposed to the doctors and insurance companies to pay for your indefinite care, then you should consider a Living Will. If you don't want to live indefinitely in a vegetative state, with no brain activity, then you should consider a Living Will. And, most importantly, by executing a Living Will, you are taking that horrible, albeit, hopefully remote decision, off of your loved one's shoulders.

The second part of the Advance Medical Directive is the Medical Power of Attorney. The Medical Power of Attorney is much like the General or Specific Power of Attorney, except that the principal is appointing an individual to direct their health care decisions should the principal be unable to do so by reason of incapacitation.

With the Medical Power of Attorney, the agent, or attorney-in-fact, as they are also called, has the ability to assist in the decision making process as to your medical care. Doctors can confer with your agent and release records to them in harmony with the Health Information Portability and Protection Act.

Alternatively, if you have not named an agent in a Medical Power of Attorney, that person would have to petition the circuit court to become appointed guardian of your person or conservator of your estate to have the authority to assist you your medical affairs while incapacitated. The petitions for guardian and conservatorship are time consuming, expensive, and the last thing your loved ones want to be doing while you are in dire straits.

CHAPTER 6:
GENERAL
DURABLE POWER OF ATTORNEY

A power of attorney is a legal document in which the grantor, or principal, grants to someone, known as the agent, the power to act as his/her "attorney-in-fact", authorizing the agent to act on his/her behalf in regards to legal or business matters.

A power of attorney may be "specific" or "limited" to one specified act or time, or it may be "general." Under the common law, a specific power of attorney becomes ineffective if its grantor dies or becomes "incapacitated," meaning unable to grant such a power, because of physical injury or mental illness.

However, under a General Durable Power of Attorney, the grantor specifies that the power of attorney will continue to be effective even if the grantor becomes incapacitated. Hence, the power of attorney endures incapacitation and is not specific to a particular act.

When first executed, a General Durable Power of Attorney can be a document of convenience. If you are literally too lazy to get up out of your Lazyboy – you can send your agent to the bank to sign documents. If you go on a business trip, and of course, that's when the refinance settlement on your home was set- your agent can sign on your behalf.

A power of attorney is generally made effective immediately upon the execution of the document, even if the principal is fully competent and able to manage their own affairs. Executing the power of attorney document does not relinquish the principal's power to manage their affairs, rather, it grants authority to the agent to be able to act on behalf of the principal as well. As long as the principal is competent the power of attorney can be revoked or replaced at any time.

The best person to name as your agent varies from person to person. Often I advise a close family member — preferably one who lives nearby. Most attorneys and financial advisors do not want the added responsibility given in a power of attorney, nor is it cost effective to pay an hourly fee to handle routine tasks like paying bills.

Naming joint agents, which is allowed only in some states, is one way to provide checks and balances. Or you can appoint another person, like an attorney, an accountant or a family friend, to supervise the arrangement.

With a power of attorney, the agent has a duty of fidelity to the grantor, commonly referred to as fiduciary duties. This duty of fidelity means that the agent can only act on behalf of the stated interests of the grantor, and not for purposes of self-dealing. Embezzling moneys, for instance, is actionable at law, not only as a criminal offense, but in the case of an agent absconding with funds obtained through the use of a power of attorney, also actionable via a civil suit for breach of fiduciary duty.

Often, it is imperative for adult children with aging parents to be named as agents under a power of attorney signed by their parents.

Again, it is a document of convenience to begin, but a General Durable Power of Attorney transforms into a document of absolute necessity should you become incapacitated. If mom becomes incapacitated, or gets on the slippery slope of dementia, for instance, how can she sign any documents for her care at the assisted living facility, or pay her mortgage? The catch-22 of it is this: if you become incapacitated, it's too late to execute a power of attorney. As such, it is important to execute a General Durable Power of Attorney with a view toward the inevitable need for its use when you become incapacitated, either by old age and infirmity, or by some acute incident, such as a car accident.

Alternatively, if you have not named an agent in a General Durable Power of Attorney, that person would have to petition the circuit court to become appointed guardian of your person or conservator of your estate to have the authority to assist you your business and legal affairs while incapacitated. As I mentioned in Chapter 5, petitions for guardian and conservatorship are time consuming, expensive, and the last thing your loved ones want to be doing while you are incapacitated.

When an individual lacks capacity and there is no valid power of attorney in place authorizing someone else to manage their financial affairs, the only resort is a legal guardianship and/or conservatorship proceeding, wherein the individual is declared incapacitated and a guardian or conservator petitions the court and is appointed to manage their property and personal needs.

There are huge drawbacks in having to resort to a guardianship and conservatorship proceeding, however, including the time and cost of the proceeding and the emotional toll on family.

It is not unusual for a guardianship and conservatorship proceeding to cost more than $15,000 to cover attorney's fees, the cost of the mandatory court evaluator (a Guardian ad litem appointed by the court to interview all interested parties and report the findings to the court), and bonding fees. There are often additional fees for the Guardian ad litem and other court-appointed professionals. Moreover, there are annual costs for court examiners (court appointees who review yearly accounts prepared by the guardian), attorneys or accountants who assist in preparing the annual accountings, annual bond premiums, and the possibility of commissions awarded to guardians and conservators for the faithful performance of their fiduciary duties.

FINAL THOUGHTS:

The advice given in this book is not meant to serve as legal advice and should not be relied upon without consideration of your own fact pattern. All estates should be scrutinized individually, and no estate planning practitioner should approach a client with a cookie-cutter approach to an estate. I advise that everyone seek legal counsel when planning for their estate.

In this age of the internet, it is very easy to get lost in the world of google searches. You will find that there are countless different types of trusts, with different names and purposes, and your head may spin. It is very easy to get lost and think you understand a core estate planning principle when in fact, you are misguided or misinformed altogether.

My thought is this: you have worked tirelessly throughout your entire life to build up your financial wealth. Why try and save a few hundred dollars and prepare a will or trust from an internet form and risk, literally, all that you have gained, to taxes, and legal proceedings?

That being said, it is better to have something in place, rather than nothing. In fact, that is the purpose of a will, as previously discussed. A will is meant to serve as the catch-net for your estate, and make sure that nothing slips through the cracks into the land of intestacy and court appointed administration of your estate.

Lastly, I always joke with my clients: "A Will or Trust can always be amended, because your estate plan is not etched into stone until you are."

www.ingramcontent.com/pod-product-compliance
Lightning Source LLC
Chambersburg PA
CBHW040259220526
45473CB00002B/527